Rural Teens and Animal Raising:
Large and Small Pets

Title List

Getting Ready for the Fair: Crafts, Projects, and Prize-Winning Animals

Growing Up on a Farm: Responsibilities and Issues

Migrant Youth: Falling Between the Cracks

Rural Crime and Poverty: Violence, Drugs, and Other Issues

Rural Teens and Animal Raising: Large and Small Pets

Rural Teens and Nature: Conservation and Wildlife Rehabilitation

Rural Teens on the Move:
Cars, Motorcycles, and Off-Road Vehicles

Teen Life Among the Amish and Other Alternative Communities:
Choosing a Lifestyle

Teen Life on Reservations and in First Nation Communities:
Growing Up Native

Teen Minorities in Rural North America: Growing Up Different

Teens and Rural Education: Opportunities and Challenges

Teens and Rural Sports: Rodeos, Horses, Hunting, and Fishing

Teens Who Make a Difference in Rural Communities:
Youth Outreach Organizations and Community Action

Rural Teens and Animal Raising:
Large and Small Pets

by Joyce Libal

Mason Crest Publishers

Philadelphia

Mason Crest Publishers Inc.
370 Reed Road
Broomall, Pennsylvania 19008
(866) MCP-BOOK (toll free)
www.masoncrest.com

First printing
1 2 3 4 5 6 7 8 9 10
ISBN 978-1-4222-0011-7 (series)

Library of Congress Cataloging-in-Publication Data

Libal, Joyce.
  Rural teens and animal raising : large and small pets / by Joyce Libal.
    p. cm. — (Rural youth)
  Includes index.
  ISBN 978-1-4222-0024-7
  1. Pets. 2. Pets--Social aspects. 3. Teenagers. 4. Rural conditions. I. Title.
II. Series.
  SF411.5L53 2006
  636.088'7—dc22
                                    2005004475

Cover and interior design by MK Bassett-Harvey.
Produced by Harding House Publishing Service, Inc.
www.hardinghousepages.com

Cover image design by Peter Spires Culotta.
Cover photography by iStock Photography (Leeuwtje,
   Levgenia Tikhonova, Steve Mann, and Salaam del Rosario).
Printed in Malaysia by Phoenix Press.

The information contained in this book should be considered a general guide. More inclusive information should be sought before adopting or caring for any pet. Injuries, including bites, scrapes, and other wounds, can occur when working with any of the animals described in this book. Animals can acquire parasites or become infected with various diseases, some of which can affect humans. Use care with all animals. Seek medical attention for all wounds, suspected parasites, and illnesses.

Contents

Introduction **6**

1. Discover Your Ideal Pet **9**

2. Of a Feather **19**

3. Down the Rabbit Trail **33**

4. From Sheep and Goats to Alpacas and Llamas **49**

5. Here Piggy Piggy **63**

6. Miniature to Grand: Horses, Ponies, and Donkeys **71**

7. Changing Circumstances **83**

Further Reading **90**

For More Information **91**

Glossary **92**

Index **94**

Picture Credits **95**

Author & Consultant Biographies **96**

Introduction

by Celeste Carmichael

Results of a survey published by the Kellogg Foundation reveal that most people consider growing up in the country to be idyllic. And it's true that growing up in a rural environment does have real benefits. Research indicates that families in rural areas consistently have more traditional values, and communities are more closely knit. Rural youth spend more time than their urban counterparts in contact with agriculture and nature. Often youth are responsible for gardens and farm animals, and they benefit from both their sense of responsibility and their understanding of the natural world. Studies also indicate that rural youth are more engaged in their communities, working to improve society and local issues. And let us not forget the psychological and aesthetic benefits of living in a serene rural environment!

The advantages of rural living cannot be overlooked—but neither can the challenges. Statistics from around the country show that children in a rural environment face many of the same difficulties that are typically associated with children living in cities, and they fare worse than urban kids on several key indicators of positive youth development. For example, rural youth are more likely than their urban counterparts to use drugs and alcohol. Many of the problems facing rural youth are exacerbated by isolation, lack of jobs (for both parents and teens), and lack of support services for families in rural communities.

When most people hear the word "rural," they instantly think "farms." Actually, however, less than 12 percent of the population in rural areas make their livings through agriculture. Instead, service jobs are the top industry in rural North America. The lack of opportunities for higher paying jobs can trigger many problems: persistent poverty, lower educational standards, limited access to health care, inadequate housing, underemployment of teens, and lack of extracurricular possibilities. Additionally, the lack of—or in some cases surge of—diverse populations in rural communities presents its own set of challenges for youth and communities. All these concerns lead to the greatest threat to rural communities: the mass exodus of the post–high school population. Teens relocate for educational, recreational, and job opportunities, leaving their hometown indefinitely deficient in youth capital.

This series of books offers an in-depth examination of both the pleasures and challenges for rural youth. Understanding the realities is the first step to expanding the options for rural youth and increasing the likelihood of positive youth development.

CHAPTER 1
Discover Your Ideal Pet

If you are an urban dweller, you are probably familiar with dogs and cats—human beings' most popular animal companions. Dogs and cats are incredibly varied and highly adaptable, which in many cases makes them suitable pets for people who live in small, urban spaces. For rural dwellers, however, access to the great outdoors opens the world of pet ownership to all kinds of possibilities. Though many people in rural areas have dogs and cats, there's also a wide array of other animals. Some of these animals you may not generally think of as pets at all, but in rural settings they can make great animal companions.

Where you live is an important factor in determining the perfect pet. From cats and dogs to rats and ferrets, rural teens often adopt the same kinds of animals as urban teens. But when rural teens have enough outdoor space and are not bound by *zoning laws* restricting livestock ownership, farm animals are sometimes chosen. No matter what type of animal one chooses, however, pet ownership is a big responsibility that requires careful consideration, planning, preparation, and commitment. Most teens find that caring for a pet offers numerous rewards, but whether your pet is small, large, common, or rare, it will have needs that must be fulfilled.

First Steps to Pet Ownership

Animals should never be adopted simply on impulse or to satisfy curiosity or ego. Pets are not to be used as a *status symbol*. As the holiday *wanes*, the animals lose their baby appeal, and the reality of the responsibilities of pet ownership set in, countless Easter chicks and bunnies are surrendered to animal shelters. Thousands of cute puppies and kittens suffer the same fate after being featured gifts for birthdays and Christmas.

When deciding if a pet is right for you, ask yourself why you want to add an animal to your life. There are many good reasons for pet ownership. Most pets enjoy a romp outdoors, providing exercise opportunities to the owner. Pets also offer companionship, and they can be great at raising spirits when their owners are in the dumps.

But let's not kid ourselves. There are drawbacks to consider as well. For one thing, animals need consistent daily care. Rural teens in North America often have extensive daily commutes to school and other activities. It is not unusual for some students to mount buses as early as 6:30 A.M. for long trips to school. These individuals must weigh their desire for a pet against the fact that they'll have to rise early enough to care for it before the bus arrives. Many students participate in after-school activities such as sports, clubs, and marching bands. Luckily, pets can usually adjust to their owner's schedule, but the pet's basic needs must be met. Water, for example, must always be available, no matter how busy the pet's owner becomes. This may not be as simple as just giving the pet fresh water in the morning. During the winter in a northern climate, an outdoor pet's water supply will freeze and need to be replaced at adequate intervals. Hectic schedules and *inclement* weather make it necessary for many teens to make arrangements with family members to care for pets in their absence *before* deciding on pet ownership. And pets deserve more than a brief visit to deliver food and water in the morning and evening. Like you, pets also have exercise, grooming, and health-care needs. Just as important, they need companionship.

What Animal Suits You Best?

When thinking about getting a pet, consider how different animals might fit your personality and lifestyle. If you only have limited time to spend with a pet, don't pick an animal that will need lots of time and personal attention. If you hate being outside, pick a pet that likes to spend most of its time indoors. If you or members of your family have allergies, you must spend time with the type of animal you are considering before committing to take it home. If other pets already live in your household, think about their compatibility and how they might accept a new arrival. Many animals will enjoy, or at least tolerate, each other if introduced gradually and with careful supervision. But some animals should never be left together when unattended. For example, rabbits and birds just don't mix with dogs and cats. To dogs and cats, your beloved pet rabbit or bird might look an awful lot like dinner.

Dogs need lots of attention.

Housing is another important thing to consider as you think about getting a pet. If your pet will be housed outdoors, you will need to have a barn, shed, or other secure shelter before bringing the pet home. Certain animals also must have access to pastures. Does your family have enough grassland for this purpose, and can that area be fenced? Some animals are expensive to purchase, house, and feed, so family finances may be an important factor in deciding whether or not to acquire a pet.

Selecting a Healthy Pet

Once you have decided to get a pet, you will have to carefully choose the exact animal you want. The animal's health should be one of your first considerations. Depending on the type of animal you want to get, you will have to look for specific health characteristics associated with that breed. However, there are some general health

Asking All the Right Questions

While observing the animal's behavior, ask the following questions of the breeder, current owner, or present staff:

How old is the animal and what is its breed's average life expectancy?

Where did it come from?

Why was it brought here? (if the animal is in a shelter)

How does it respond to other animals?

How does it respond to people such as children and strangers?

Is it housebroken?

What veterinary care has it received, has it received appropriate testing, and is it updated on all its shots?

Has it been spayed or neutered?

Will it require any specialized or unusual care?

Does this animal require an experienced owner?

Where can I find more information about this type/breed of animal, including the average size of the breed?

guidelines that apply to most animals. For example, a healthy animal will usually appear attentive to its surroundings. A sleepy, *listless*, and unresponsive animal may be in poor health. A healthy animal's eyes will be bright and free of discharge. Its fur or feathers

Even small animals will have many needs to consider.

will look clean and full, without thin or bald spots. You should also inspect the animal's ears for cleanliness, and make sure there is no discharge from the nose. Pet the animal to be sure it is free of bumps and sores. Part the fur to look at the skin; be certain it is clean and does not have *lesions* or a scaly surface. Animals should look well fed but not fat. Even pet pigs should not be obese. If there is evidence of diarrhea in the pen or on an animal's body, do not purchase a pet, even a healthy-looking one, from this location. Even if only one animal appears unhealthy, all the animals could be adversely affected. Be sure to take a close look at the facility from where you are considering getting your pet. Is it clean, and do all of the animals look healthy and well cared for?

Inspecting a potential pet gives you an opportunity to observe not only its physical health but also some aspects of its personality. Both breed personality and the individual animal's personality will be important considerations as you choose your new companion. Consider how much time you will have to work on developing your relationship with your pet. Then consider whether the animal is already friendly, or if it will require much care and patience on your

Finding a Vet

One of the most important people in your pet's life will be her vet. Take the time to educate yourself about your pet's veterinary care needs and to find the best-qualified vet in your area.

Don't wait until you need a vet to look for one. Ask friends, breeders, and shelter workers for recommendations. Visit the facility: Is it clean? Are the workers friendly and show they care for your pet? How many vets and technicians are in the practice? Are the vets board certified? Are emergency services available?

Not all vets can treat every kind of animal. Keep in mind that if you have a "farm animal" as a pet, you will probably need a large-animal vet. These caregivers see patients in their offices like other vets, but they also make house calls so you don't have to take your pet to her. They are specially trained in the treatment of these types of animals.

If you're partial to flying pets, you may have to find a vet who specializes in exotic pets. Some, but not all, small-animal vets care for birds.

Your pet depends on you to find her the best care possible. If you're comfortable with the vet and her services, chances are so will your pet—well, as comfortable as she can be about going to the doctor.

part to gain its trust. Does it seem inquisitive and interested in you? Is it playful? Does it respond when offered a treat? Are any signs of aggression present, or is the animal overly timid and fearful?

Animal Care 101

Once you get your pet home, the real fun—and the real work—begins. As you play with your pet, you will begin learning about its specific needs. All animals must be handled thoughtfully. Pay close attention to how the pet responds to different situations. An animal will teach you its favorite ways to be touched, the treats it likes best, and which toys interest it most.

All pets must have food and water to grow properly and be healthy. Workers at a local feed or pet store can help you select products that are specially formulated to contain the correct vitamins and minerals for your pet. Most animals appreciate having their diet supplemented with occasional treats. Never feed alcohol, caffeine, or similar substances to animals. The same is true of chocolate and sugary treats. Spicy foods and rhubarb leaves should also be avoided. Check breed information for other things that might cause your pet intestinal distress.

Animals require adequate shelter from wind, rain, snow, and too much sun. Electrical wires and outlets, as well as telephone cords, can pose a hazard to indoor pets. Cover outlets with plastic, child-proof covers, and place wires and cords under carpets wherever possible.

Keep coops, cages, and animal yards clean to ward off sickness and parasites. Remove excrement daily, and do not allow stale food or water to remain in pens. Immunizations against specific diseases are necessary. Grooming helps maintain good health and comfort—in general, the hairier the pet, the more time must be spent washing and combing the pet's coat.

Pets and Pesticides Don't Mix

Never allow animals to feed on plants that have recently been sprayed with pesticides, insecticides, or chemical fertilizers. Your pet can develop diarrhea, other serious symptoms, or possibly even die if exposed to these substances.

Some pets need specific training. Animals housed in the home become better family members when they are housebroken, and animals that are taken for walks, including large animals, need to learn to walk manageably on leads.

Knowing the basics of pet ownership is essential to having a relationship that is safe, healthy, and rewarding to both you and your pet. Many of the most important details of pet ownership, however, are determined by the specific type of pet you have. Although all pets have basic requirements like food and water, knowing the specific things your pet will need to be healthy and happy may require a good deal of research and effort on your part. You may be surprised to learn how involved a pet's needs can be, especially in a rural area where pets might be exposed to harsh elements or predators. For instance, in rural areas, birds from chickens to peacocks can be beautiful, interesting, and even useful pets, but they also have special needs that must be considered and provided for.

CHAPTER 2
Of a Feather

Both in rural and urban areas, birds make popular pets. Unlike caged finches, parakeets, lovebirds, and other small birds commonly kept in houses and apartments, larger members of the *avian* world are often favored by rural families. Though chickens raised commercially for eggs and meat have short lives (sometimes only a couple of months), a small flock of pet chickens can provide years of family interest and enjoyment. But chickens are by no means the only type of birds kept in rural areas; poultry of every type—including quail, pheasants, peacocks, and guinea fowl—are relatively common and can be ordered from catalogues or over the Internet. When ordered in this manner, baby birds will usually arrive by mail at your local post office or be delivered directly to your door.

Get Ready for the Big Day

Baby birds of all types are delicate and require a great deal of specialized care. When birds hatch in natural surroundings, they spend their first days or weeks of life huddled under a parent's body for safety and warmth. If you purchase baby birds at a store or through the mail, they will arrive minus a protective parent. Their new protective parent is you, and you will have to provide a safe, warm place for the little birds to live and grow. To do this, you will need to assemble a brooder, a small, enclosed, heated area where the birds will be kept.

Young birds have thin and immature feathers, so your brooder will need to be equipped with a heat source (usually a special lightbulb) to keep your little birds warm. Place the heat source so the temperature beneath it remains at an appropriate level for the type of bird. For chickens, begin with a temperature of 95 degrees Fahrenheit (35 degrees Celsius). For ducks and geese, begin with a temperature 86 degrees Fahrenheit (30 degrees Celsius). Each week, move the light higher to decrease the temperature by about five degrees. Continue using a heat source until babies are well feathered.

The brooder should not be too large, but it needs to be big enough for chicks to move away from the heat source when desired. Since your baby birds will bunch up for warmth, it is a good idea to make the brooder round. This way, there will be no corners where your baby birds will cluster, which can lead to suffocation. Even if your brooder is square, you can place a round corral made of corrugated cardboard inside and remove it when the birds are larger.

Fresh water and feed must be available at all times. Commercial food and water containers are best for chicks, but ducks and geese must be able to submerge their entire head. As soon as your baby birds arrive, dip each one's beak gently in the water to help the birds

A chick is not a cute Easter decoration. It requires lots of tender loving care.

understand where the water is and to hydrate them after their journey. Feed the appropriate commercial starter for the poultry you are raising. If you are raising chickens, you can move them on to *pullet* grower when they are about six weeks old. At five or six months, switch them to laying feed.

One sometimes-unpleasant aspect of bird ownership is the need to keep the bird's vent clear. So what's a vent? It's your bird's butt! Sometimes birds' vents get clogged with pasty droppings. This unpleasant situation can get serious quickly, resulting in illness and even death. When you notice dried droppings stuck to your birds' bottoms, remove them by gently dabbing with warm water on a moistened cloth.

Use dry bedding and keep it free of droppings. Sawdust is often a poor choice of bedding material for baby birds because they may try to eat it, and the close proximity of the heat source can be a fire risk. Simple dirt or sand is usually a better choice. Newspaper is too slippery; the little birds can fall and damage their delicate legs.

Diseases spread easily from chicken to chicken.

Older Birds

If purchasing older birds, first observe the flock and the facility in which it's kept. Poultry should be moving around with ease. Water and feed should be available in clean dishes. Coops should be well cared for. If you notice birds sitting on the sidelines with feathers puffed out and eyes closed—signs of illness in birds—do not purchase pets from this facility. Avoid all birds if any members of the flock are coughing or sneezing. If you notice any of these symptoms in your own flock, isolate the infected birds immediately. Diseases can spread through a flock quickly, and as sad as it is, it may become necessary to kill birds that seem very sick to keep the rest of the flock safe from infection. After death, the bodies of birds *culled* due to illness should be burned or buried away from where you house the rest of the birds.

Once you have approved of the flock and facility, take a closer look at the individuals you are considering. Never catch, pick up, or carry any bird by its legs or feet! Be certain the beak closes properly. Birds should be clear-eyed and have clean, smooth feathers. Nostrils must also be clear and free of discharge. A brightly colored, smooth-looking comb is a sign of good health. Look at the bird's vent. There should not be stains or feces surrounding this area.

Coops and Cages

The luckiest of fowl aficionados will already have access to a barn or small shed that can be converted to a coop. It is important for the coop to be *vermin* proof, and in this case vermin includes cats and dogs as well as snakes, rodents, and other wild animals. If you already have a building large enough to house your flock, simply provide appropriate roosts and nesting boxes. (Ducks and geese do not use either of these.) A small door with a lock can be opened in the morning to allow birds free access to a fenced area during the day and closed in the evening to provide safety from predators at night.

Bird housing doesn't have to be elaborate. If you have just a few chickens, for example, they will happily accept a modest home like an elevated wooden cage within a fenced enclosure. Birds with full access to a yard will spend nearly their whole day outside, just returning to their cage at night.

A Healthy Flock

Keep baby birds out of drafts. To avoid many diseases, excessive feather plucking, and pecking at each other, give the flock plenty of

Healthy chickens
need plenty of
space and fresh air.

room for exercise and provide a constant supply of feed. Make sure feeders are long enough and there are enough of them to allow at least half of the flock to eat at the same time. As chickens grow, raise feeders off the floor so birds do not have to bend far to get food. This can help prevent leg injury in some breeds. Using a commercial feed that is fortified with the vitamins necessary for whichever type of fowl you are raising will help maintain flock health. Whenever possible, treat your birds to fresh greens. They'll happily rid your household of carrot peelings and other vegetable matter.

To avoid mites, lice, and many other pests, keep the flock away from other birds and clean the coop regularly. Remember also to clean all roosts. Good sanitary practices help *stave* off pests like flatworms and roundworms. Bird droppings make coops very dusty; always wear a dust mask or respirator when cleaning.

All Birds Molt

At some point each year, your beautiful flock is going to look a little ratty. This is because birds have an "out with the old and in with the new" policy regarding their wardrobes. All of those lovely feathers will drop out and be replaced with new ones. Exactly when this happens is determined by the earth's natural cycle. As winter turns to spring, the days begin to get longer, the weather grows warmer, the humidity changes, and your birds will molt. Don't worry; feathers will be lost gradually so members of the flock will never be completely nude. Continue to care for the birds, making sure the coop and yard are clean and plenty of water and feed are available, and your birds will be back in tip-top *plumage* in a matter of weeks.

Egg Production

Your avian pets can be fun and beautiful, but they can also be useful. Many bird owners love being able to collect eggs from their flock. Chickens lay more eggs than other types of fowl. Healthy hens will usually begin laying eggs regularly and easily at about five months, provided they are getting about twelve hours of light daily. Natural daylight can be supplemented with lights inside the chicken coop. Cold temperatures also have a negative effect on egg production. Male birds are not necessary for egg production; they are only necessary if babies are desired. Sometimes hens get broody. That's when they stop laying eggs and are reluctant to move off the nest.

Provide nesting boxes filled with hay or straw. A plastic egg may be placed in the nest for extra encouragement. Egg production decreases as hens get older. Expect an increasing loss of the yellow pigment in legs and beaks as egg production continues. Collect eggs at least twice a day, wash them well, and refrigerate immediately. The yolks of home-raised eggs will be darker than those purchased at the grocery store, especially if they come from *free-range* birds.

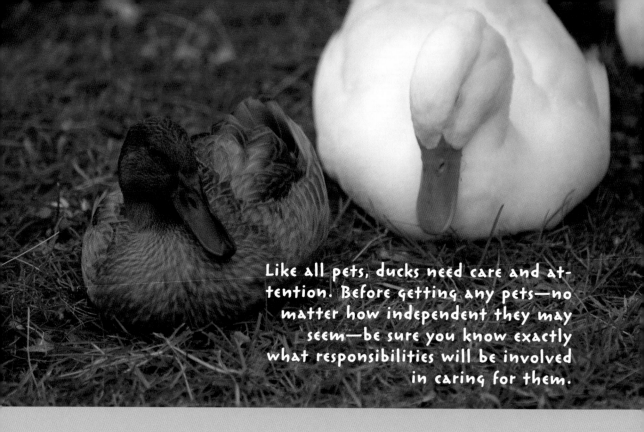

Like all pets, ducks need care and attention. Before getting any pets—no matter how independent they may seem—be sure you know exactly what responsibilities will be involved in caring for them.

More About Ducks and Geese

Ducks will be happiest if they have access to water for swimming (for some species it is essential), but geese don't seem to mind going without it. Both ducks and geese are hardy, easy to raise, great *foragers*, and able to thrive under a variety of conditions. Geese are capable of protecting themselves from a variety of predators and can be particularly long-lived, sometimes reaching the ripe old age of thirty.

Grass and weeds are among the favorite foods of ducks and geese, but they would also love to eat most of the young vegetable plants growing in the garden. Be warned, therefore, that although these birds can be free ranging, you must fence them off from plants you want to protect. Insects are also an enjoyable entrée, and some owners allow pet ducks and geese to comb mature gardens for slugs,

Ducks enjoy a place to swim.

snails, and similar pests. Provide a constant supply of fresh water (remember that containers need to be large enough to allow these birds to dip their heads) and feed even if your flock is allowed to forage.

Both ducks and geese produce large eggs and prefer to nest on or near the floor. Their eggs can be used interchangeably with chicken eggs in all recipes, but you will have to reduce the number used because of size. There can be a vast difference in the number of eggs produced per year depending on duck breed. Muscovy ducks lay only forty to forty-five eggs per year; Khaki Campbells can produce between 300 and 350.

Pigeon Pets

Chickens, ducks, and geese are some of the most common birds kept by young people in rural areas, but there are plenty of other outdoor birds from which one could choose. Steve, a youth in Wisconsin,

The Down Side of Pet Geese

You may have heard that geese make good watchdogs. That's because they're often noisy and aggressive. One goose can be an ideal pet, but these birds usually live in flocks. They are social creatures, and a single goose may become very lonely. Many families choose to keep at least three geese (one gander and two females is the common trio). However, even in rural areas where the geese have plenty of space, three are sometimes overwhelming. The same aggression the gander uses to protect his bird family from predators can be intimidating to humans. When in defense and attack mode, these large birds sometimes run at people, and their bite and powerful, flapping wings can be painful.

Before adopting these pets, also consider the mess. Just three geese can produce a surprising amount of manure. Everywhere your geese range, from the banks of a family pond to your home's front doorstep, this "evidence" will be left behind.

kept pigeons for twelve years. Steve found Butch and Bluebell highly interesting, entertaining, and rewarding.

Like most pigeons, Butch and Bluebell mated for life. They were not only loyal to each other, however. They were also quite loyal to Steve. Butch and Bluebell had strong *homing instincts*, a trait common to most pigeons, so they were allowed to fly free on most days. When Steve boarded the school bus in the mornings, Butch and

Pigeons prefer flat surfaces.

Bluebell would often fly down the road after the bus. But they would always return before the bus had traveled a mile.

If you are considering keeping pigeons as pets, be aware that rather than perching on tree branches like many other birds, pigeons prefer to hang out on flat surfaces. For Steve, the roof of the pigsty served this purpose nicely, and Butch and Bluebell were usually hanging around there when he returned from school. Another thing to keep in mind about pigeons is that a mated pair can produce as many as fifteen young per year. If you don't want a flock of pigeons (something many people find messy and noisy), you will have to remove the eggs. Steve allowed some of Butch and Bluebell's eggs to hatch, but his family ate most of them. Nevertheless, the flock became significantly larger over the years.

A pheasant cock has colorful plumage, while the hen is more drab.

If you allow your pet pigeons to become parents, you will notice that the male and female share equally in squab rearing. Typically, the female lays two eggs, then the prospective parents take turns sitting on them to keep the eggs warm. About eighteen days later, the naked babies peck their way into the world. They will stretch their skinny necks upward and squeak for food. When the babies feed, their whole heads will disappear into the parent's open mouths. Deep within the adult bird's *crop*, the babies locate pigeon milk. Squabs become adults very quickly. At about one month old, they already have feathers and begin to leave the nest. Within six months, they, too, will be producing the main ingredient of pigeon omelets.

Big Birds Can Equal Bad Pets

Emus, rheas, and ostriches are the largest of birds. Raised for meat, leather, feathers, and oil, they do not usually make good pets. Even fenced, these birds have been known to peck or occasionally snatch an earring from a passerby. Long legs allow these flightless birds to run very fast and to deliver powerful blows.

Although chickens, ducks, and geese are by far the most common outdoor birds kept in rural areas, they are by no means the only birds to choose from. If you are interested in fancy plumage, there are many rare breeds of chickens, ducks, or geese to choose from, but you could also consider partridges, quails, or pheasants, which come in a wide variety of types and colors. For something even more unusual, you could choose guineas. Then, of course, there are peafowl, long celebrated for their decorative plumage and the cock's impressive tail.

Keeping birds can provide you with a wide variety of rewarding experiences, but if you are looking for a pet who will be more of a companion, outdoor fowl may not be the best option for you. Many young people look for a pet who will be a little more cuddly than your average bird. If you are looking for a pet who is relatively easy to care for, can adapt to an outdoor or indoor environment, and can be an animal companion but can also tolerate having time alone, a rabbit might be a good option for you.

CHAPTER 3
Down the Rabbit Trail

Though rabbits were first *domesticated* for meat and pelts, today millions of them are kept as pets in North America. In rural areas, it is easy to house them in outdoor hutches, yet many owners prefer to keep their rabbits inside the home. Indoors or outdoors, rabbits make ideal pets. These sweet creatures take up very little space and can be trained to use a litter box. Cute and playful bunnies are available in colors and sizes to suit any taste. Local county and state fairs offer an excellent opportunity to view many breeds.

Picking the Ideal Rabbit

You can expect a healthy rabbit to be part of your family for seven to ten years, so choose your rabbit carefully. A male rabbit has scent glands on its chin and may rub them on items to mark its territory. Sexually mature male rabbits often urinate in various areas for the same reason; *neutering* usually discourages this habit, but the surgery can be dangerous for some rabbits. If you would rather not deal with these situations, select a female.

Inspect the mouth to be certain there is proper contact between upper and lower teeth when the jaw is closed. Rabbit teeth grow throughout the creature's life; teeth that meet correctly grind each other down naturally when the animal chews food. Avoid selecting a rabbit with buckteeth, also called a malocclusion; there's no such thing as braces for rabbits. Instead, the owner must monitor tooth growth, and a veterinarian has to manually grind the teeth down on a regular basis. Without this extra care, a rabbit with a malocclusion will eventually have deformed teeth that prevent it from eating.

In the wild, rabbits are animals of prey. Therefore, most rabbits are naturally skittish and will scratch their way out of frightening situations. Although rabbits are relatively easy to tame, it won't happen without effort on your part. Socialize your bunny by taking it out of its cage and playing with it daily. Some rabbits can be cuddly, but many do not like to be held. Don't despair if your bunny resists cuddling. Instead, sit down and encourage it to lay beside you as you gently stroke its fur.

Inside or Outside?

Many rabbit owners choose to house their pet outdoors. An outdoor hutch should include shelter from rain and wind. Damp or drafty

Rabbits enjoy fresh air and a chance to nibble grass and weeds. However, be sure to closely supervise your rabbit's outings, as it can easily run away. Rabbits do not come when called! And they are easy prey for dogs, hawks, and owls.

conditions are unhealthy for rabbits. While some sun is desirable, the pet needs to avoid too much exposure. If you are good at woodworking or can get help from a parent or friend, it is possible to build your own rabbit hutch. Here are design ideas to get you started:

- To discourage visits by rats and mice, use a combination of wood and wire fencing to build an elevated rabbit home.

- Either 2 x 4- or 4 x 4-inch lumber is a good choice for legs.

- A wire bottom allows excrement to fall through. This makes it easier to clean the cage and helps to discourage disease.

- Build the walls and wooden top of the enclosure so the pen has a slanted roof, and cover it with shingles to make it waterproof.

- Enclose about half of the wall area with wood rather than fencing, or place a wooden box in the pen so your rabbit can get out of the sun. Cut a hole in the box so the rabbit can

This two-story rabbit hutch allows its inhabitants plenty of space, fresh air, and privacy, while offering easy access for cleaning.

easily enter when it desires. A box like this also provides extra protection in wet or snowy weather.

- Remember that you must be able to access all areas of the cage in order to clean it. (Weekly washing is advised. Use a disinfectant that is safe for rabbits.) One option is to place a hinged door in one side of the cage.

Thumper is a common rabbit name for a good reason—thumping a back leg is a common rabbit behavior that may be used to demand attention, warn of danger, or indicate fear. Placing a board in an all-wire cage provides a place for your rabbit to make these communications. It also gives welcome relief from the wire environment. Without it, a rabbit can develop sore feet and even *abscesses*.

If you decide to keep your rabbit indoors, you can purchase an indoor cage from almost any pet store. Even if you are going to let your rabbit roam freely around your home, having a cage provides a place that he can retreat to when he wants to be alone and feel secure. The cage should be at least three to four square feet (92 to 114 square centimeters) for most midsize rabbits. Two square feet (60 square centimeters) would be enough for a dwarf rabbit, while a giant requires five square feet (153 square centimeters). All cages should be at least fourteen inches (35.5 centimeters) tall. Of course, your rabbit will appreciate having more space if that is possible, especially if he is going to be confined to the cage most of the time.

For easy cleaning, get an indoor cage with a removable tray. If training your pet to use a litter box, select a cage that is large enough to accommodate a litter box. Place another litter box where the bunny can find it when running loose in the home. Rabbits have a natural tendency to use the same corner every time they need to relieve themselves. If the rabbit has already selected a space for this activity, it will be difficult to change its mind about the location. The easiest solution will be to place the litter box in the location the rabbit has already picked—although this may not be possible if the rabbit has decided the best place to go to the bathroom is, say, beneath your bed. Training may go faster if you put a few of the rabbit's droppings in the litter box and bring them to her attention.

Consider the placement of the cage carefully. Even indoor rabbits must avoid drafts and long exposure to direct sunlight. For these reasons, cages are usually best placed on tables and away from windows. Rabbits do not have sweat glands, so exposure to heat sources should also be avoided.

Rabbits love to chew on almost anything, so choose your rabbit's bedding material carefully. Many pet stores recommend sawdust, woodchips, or wood shavings as bedding for rabbits and most other caged animals, but beware! The naturally occurring *resins* in many types of wood can irritate your pet's eyes, skin, and respiratory system. Cedar bedding is particularly dangerous in this regard and can

Hay is often used for bedding for outdoor rabbits. During winter months, if enough hay is provided, rabbits will burrow into it, finding insulation against the cold.

actually be toxic to your rabbit. These types of bedding can also become great breeding grounds for lice, mites, and diseases. Some pet stores offer bedding alternatives made of other natural or recycled materials, but you must research the specific material carefully to make sure it is free of any chemicals, dyes, perfumes, or other potentially harmful additives, as your rabbit is likely to consume some of its bedding. Some veterinarians recommend plain black and white newspaper (no colored ink!) as the only safe option for rabbit and other small-animal bedding.

Depending on how much time your rabbit spends in its cage, an indoor rabbit may not need much bedding. Rabbits kept outdoors, however, will be dependent on their bedding to help keep them warm. They must have an adequate supply at all times, especially in the winter. For an outdoor rabbit, straw and hay might also be considered, but these materials can become very dusty and will need to be changed frequently to keep them free of urine, odors, and bacteria. Barley straw should be avoided.

A Word to the Wise Regarding Indoor Rabbits

Bunnies are inquisitive, they are endowed with a great desire to chew, and they have powerful little paws and claws. They enjoy using all of these gifts to explore their surroundings. Unsupervised rabbits in bedrooms sometimes rearrange clothing left on the floor and add their personal touch to their owner's wardrobes. If you don't want Thumper to place decorative holes in your jeans, it's best to provide constant supervision. Carpets can also suffer when rabbits are left to their own devices, and that can put family members on edge. Rabbits have a fondness for gnawing wood and shredding paper; they really will eat your homework, so keep schoolwork off the floor. Some athletic bunnies might surprise you with their leaping abilities—clothing and homework left on beds and tables may not be safe either.

Rabbits and Their Roommates

Many animals like to have members of their own species as pals. Rabbits, however, are usually loners. While it is possible to keep more than one rabbit, it can be difficult to prevent them from fighting. Young rabbits who are raised together are the most likely to get along. If you have both a male and female rabbit, *spaying* or neutering is a must to avoid unwanted litters. If you have two males, neutering will also help to avoid territorial disputes. Surgery for rabbits must be considered carefully, however, as not all rabbits respond well to the stress, and some may even die as a result.

Rabbits often prefer to be alone. However, littermates can become very attached to each other and enjoy being housed together.

If you want to have a dog or cat in addition to a rabbit, it is best to acquire the rabbit first and introduce a puppy or kitten after the rabbit is grown. Even when introduced in this manner, however, these pets should never play together unsupervised. If an adult cat already resides in the household, it may be best to keep it separated from the rabbit. Ferrets and rabbits definitely don't mix. The same is true of rabbits and large snakes.

Dwarf or Giant? Picking a Breed

Deciding on a tiny dwarf, a twenty-pound giant, or something in-between is a matter of personal taste and available space. If you want a rabbit that will practically fit into your hand, a dwarf variety will be for you. If you decide on a giant breed, don't expect to be holding it or carrying it around too much.

Dogs and rabbits can become friends—but you should always supervise their interactions.

Weighing no more than 2.5 pounds (approximately one kilogram) and available in many colors, the Netherland Dwarf is the smallest rabbit breed. In the under-three-pound (under 1.4 kilograms) category, you'll find Polish, Hotot, Britannia Petite, and Jersey Woolly rabbits. Moving just a bit larger—from three up to about nine pounds (about 1.4 to 4 kilograms)—you can consider Silver Martens, Havanas, English Spot, and Dutch Black, among others. From nine to approximately twelve pounds (approximately 4 to 5.4 kilograms), check out New Zealand White, Californian, Rexs, and Satins. If you prefer a really large rabbit, twelve to twenty pounds (5.4 to 9 kilograms), select from among the giants; Flemish Giants, Checkered Giants, and Giant Chinchillas are among your choices.

Fur type is also a matter of personal taste, and whether you want to spend time grooming your pet or wish to avoid this task as much as possible is something to consider when choosing a breed. Angora rabbits can have fur that is over three inches (over 8 centimeters) long and require a great deal of grooming to stay free of tangles and mats. Rex rabbits have a short but velvety pelt. Satin varieties and

Rabbits come in many sizes.

Chinchilla types also have lustrous coats. Rabbits don't shed fur continuously, but they do lose fur about every three to six months. Although it is not usually necessary to groom rabbits with short fur, it is a good idea to provide daily brushing when they are shedding.

Fur length and type may not be the only thing you'd like to consider when choosing your breed. Many people are attracted to the lop-eared varieties' quirky, drooping ears. And mixed-breed rabbits can have a wide variety of unusual and charming physical characteristics.

Crepuscular and Lagomorph What?

Some creatures, including certain insects, birds, and bats, are most active at twilight and just before dawn. "Crepuscular" is the word used to describe this lifestyle. Rabbits living in the wild also fall into this category. For this reason, you may find that your bunny especially enjoys playing with you in the early evening and morning hours.

Lagomorph is a word used to describe gnawing mammals that eat plants, have furry feet, and have two pairs of upper incisor teeth. Rabbits fall into this category as well.

Keeping Your Rabbit in Good Health

A constant supply of fresh, clean water is essential to your rabbit's health. A gravity-feed water bottle is best since lightweight dishes can be overturned and heavy dishes are vulnerable to contamination (rabbits often use them as toilets). Sometimes gravity-feed bottles begin to leak, so check them frequently.

The mainstay of your rabbit's diet should be a commercial pelleted food. Adding hay to the diet will provide necessary *roughage*, and when your rabbit is about five months old, fresh greens can be offered. In general, any raw vegetable you eat is safe for your rabbit when provided gradually and in moderation. Parsley, carrots

Rabbits enjoy fresh vegetables, and including a moderate amount in a rabbit's diet helps keep her healthy. Too much fresh food, however, can sometimes make a rabbit sick.

(especially the green tops), spinach, and kale are a few examples of appropriate rabbit foods. When it is free of chemicals, it is fine to provide a handful of grass from your lawn (which can include dandelion greens and clover). To most rabbits, twigs from apple trees will be a welcome treat. Fresh foods are an important part of a complete diet, but some plants are poisonous to rabbits, so consult your veterinarian about the safety of specific plants.

It is possible to get too much of a good thing, and if you see diarrhea in your rabbit's cage, something is wrong. This is often the result of too much fresh green food. Removing the greens and cutting back on the size of future servings will usually solve the problem. Diarrhea, however, can also be a symptom of more serious conditions. If diarrhea continues after removing your rabbit's green foods, look for other signs of a health problem. Do you notice bloating in your rabbit's abdominal area, and has she lost her appetite? Has her coat become dull and rough? Are her ears drooping when they are

From Scrub to Full Pedigree

The American Rabbit Breeders Association (ARBA) is the official organization charged with rabbit registration. Rabbits with registered pedigrees are top-of-the-line in the rabbit world. These purebred rabbits have colored tattoos in their ears, with the color indicating how many generations of the rabbit's family have been registered with the ARBA. Purebred rabbits are those with pedigrees that can be traced back for three or more generations.

At the opposite end of the extreme are rabbits of mixed heritage whose breed cannot be identified. These rabbits are labeled scrub. Between the two extremes you will find grade rabbits. Although the parents of these rabbits are not purebred, the rabbit's breed can still be identified.

normally upright? Rather than moving around the cage normally, is she hunched up and quiet? When your rabbit has symptoms like these, it's time to visit the vet. Make certain that your vet is well-versed in the care of rabbits. (And make sure the vet does not prescribe amoxicillin. Most vets are aware that this particular antibiotic can be toxic to rabbits.)

Colds, mites, fleas, and hairballs are other common health complications to watch for in your rabbit. A runny nose and sneezing can indicate a cold and mean you should contact your vet. To prevent colds, keep your rabbit out of drafts. An increase in ear scratching can be a symptom of mites. You should check your rabbit's ears

Knit a Rabbit Sweater or Scarf?

It's possible. Start with an Angora rabbit. Keep your furry pet clean, brush it daily, and save the fur that is removed from the brush. You can expect to collect between eleven and seventeen ounces (between 311 and 481 grams) of "wool" each year. It is also possible to shear the rabbit. After collecting the amount you desire, take the fur to a spinner who can process it into yarn. While you're saving fur, purchase a good beginner's knitting book and practice the craft. When you are confident of your knitting prowess, select a scarf or sweater pattern that suits your knitting skill. When the beautiful angora yarn is returned to you, you'll be ready to knit a special garment that can be worn with pride and treasured for a lifetime. Angora yarn is also suitable for weaving.

on a regular basis for mites, scabs, or discharge. The best way to prevent mites is through vigilant cleanliness. If your rabbit contracts mites, you will need a vet's assistance to clear up the infestation. A great deal of scratching can also be a sign of fleas, and for this, too, your vet can offer treatment options. Because rabbits self-groom as cats do, hairballs can be a problem. Swelling in the abdomen accompanied by a decrease in excrement can be an indicator of a hairball. Call your vet for a remedy. Regular exercise and the addition of hay to the diet help to prevent hairballs.

A Rather Disgusting Tidbit

Like other gnawing creatures, rabbits have two types of feces. One is soft and is sometimes eaten by the animal because it contains nutrients that help rabbits survive in the wild. The other is hard, and your rabbit knows enough to avoid it.

Exercise will not only prevent hairballs. It will also contribute to your rabbit's overall physical and emotional health. Your rabbit will love outdoor exercise in good weather, but do not leave it unattended. Providing playtime out of the cage each day will go a long way toward ensuring a long and happy life.

Rabbits can be great, cuddly companions, but many young people in rural areas have the opportunity to keep pets of much larger varieties. In urban areas, it is very unusual for young people to be able to keep an animal that is much larger than a medium-sized dog. The outdoor space available in the country, however, allows some young people to explore other four-legged creatures like sheep, goats, alpacas, and llamas.

CHAPTER 4
From Sheep and Goats to Alpacas and Llamas

Mary had a little lamb;
its fleece was white as snow.
And everywhere that Mary went,
the lamb was sure to go.

Perhaps the lamb follows Mary in the well-known nursery rhyme because these usually timid but sweet animals have a strong herding instinct. Many rural families begin with a couple of sheep as a 4-H project and end up raising a little flock. The owners of small flocks (about a half dozen sheep) often treat their ewes and ram as pets. The group multiplies quickly as ewes often give birth to twins.

49

Females are kept or sold to become breeders, while males often become market lambs (sold for meat). Of course it is possible to forgo breeding and keep a couple of sheep simply for enjoyment. Families with large acreage often use grazing animals to keep pastures from becoming overgrown. It also adds to the *pastoral* feeling of rural living to look across fields dotted with sheep, goats, horses, and other animals. Nowadays you may even see alpacas and llamas grazing peacefully in rural North America.

Raising Orphan Lambs

Many rural teens who want to raise sheep begin by adopting an orphan lamb. Ewes can be attentive mothers, but they are also notorious for abandoning their young. This usually happens because some circumstance made the ewe confused or nervous during or immediately after the birth and interfered with her bonding with the newborn lambs. Sometimes ewes will refuse to nurse more than one of a set of twins or triplets. Shepherds employ many techniques to establish a proper bond between ewes and their newborns, but when all measures fail, it becomes necessary to bottle-feed the baby with commercially made lamb milk-replacer.

When adopting a lamb, numerous considerations must be kept in mind. Playing mom to a baby *Bovidae* is fun and educational but also demanding. If your lamb is less than two weeks old when you adopt it, you'll need to give it a bottle four times each day. Begin with four ounces of lamb milk-replacer at each feeding and gradually increase to six ounces. You might notice the lamb feels warmer to the touch about five or ten minutes after it finishes the bottle. Don't be alarmed. This surprising phenomenon only lasts for about a minute and is caused by a natural dilation of capillaries in the lamb's skin.

Lambs require a great deal of care.

Beware of Wildlife

In rural areas frequented by large mammals such as bears or cougars, outdoor housing for small pets, including adult goats and sheep, must be especially sturdy. A cougar can easily jump over fences, and bears can knock susceptible cages to the ground with just a wave of the paw. Even smaller wild animals such as foxes and opossums pose a threat to small domestic animals. When your pet is out of your sight, it must be kept in a safe and secure area. Lock all outdoor pets in wooden enclosures for the night.

When your lamb is between two and three weeks old, gradually increase the ration to eight ounces. As lambs grow they develop an increasing need for water. At first, supply this via the bottle. Hay, pelleted feed, and a small amount of grain should be provided from the very beginning. Consult your veterinarian to determine the exact amount of dry feed to provide and when to begin decreasing the number of bottle feedings.

Bottle-fed lambs are more susceptible to sickness than those raised by their moms. Speak to the breeder and your veterinarian about any necessary vaccinations. All feeding equipment should be kept very clean, and care must be taken to not overfeed the youngster. The lamb should also not eat too quickly, so the size of the hole in the bottle's nipple is important. Diarrhea is cause for an immediate call to the vet, who may recommend cutting back on the amount fed, providing an occasional feeding of plain water or another

Goats make friendly and gentle pets (although they often like to nibble on sleeves, shoelaces, and braids!).

substance, and administering a few teaspoons of Pepto-Bismol. A bloated lamb also necessitates telephoning the veterinarian. Overfeeding becomes less of a concern as the lamb ages. Your pet will be happy to take a bottle from you indefinitely, so, as the "mom," you must decide when it's time to **wean** the animal. Remember that all changes in feed should be gradual.

Goats

Like sheep, goats are happiest with at least one roommate of their own kind. When that is not possible, they will accept other animals as pasture and stablemates. Goats are **gregarious**, curious, sometimes stubborn, and usually quite hardy. Both sheep and goats can be friendly companions and will be happy to supply fertilizer in the form of manure for the garden. Unlike sheep, which are grazers,

Straw makes good bedding for goats. It soaks up moisture from the floor and provides insulation, keeping goats warm, dry, and comfortable.

goats are browsers—animals that move frequently while eating twigs and leaves from bushes and small trees. Goats can consume a wide variety of plants. Be aware, however, that they will not discriminate between weeds and valuable landscaping shrubs, and the little acrobats will stand on their hind legs to reach up as far as possible to get the plant "goodies."

Many people who raise goats do so for their milk. Nubians, Toggenburgs, Alpines, and Saanens are among the most popular goat breeds raised for milk. The curious-looking, usually earless La Mancha is another milking breed. If dairy products are your goal, realize that goats must be bred periodically to sustain milk production. You will either have to keep a billy goat (a male, also called a buck) along with nanny (a female, also called a doe) or locate a boyfriend for her within a convenient drive of your home. Do not have the doe bred until she is at least a year old. Milking must be performed every twelve hours, which can be a real downer for busy teen schedules. You will need to locate adoptive parents for the kids (baby goats) or else you will have a herd within a short time.

Those who have more than one goat must guard against premature mating by separating does from bucks by about three months of age. In general, the sexual desires and habits of mature bucks are such that the females make better pets. Billy goats have musk glands that produce an odor female goats find delightful but most pet owners would rather avoid. It is possible to have these glands removed, and if you want a male kid as a pet only, you can have him neutered while he is still young, before he matures sexually, in which case he will not develop musk glands.

If you like to knit, crochet, or weave and want to raise goats for yarn, check out Angoras. These white, curly haired goats can be sheared to produce mohair. If pasture area is limited or you just want a really small and very cute pet, consider pygmy goats. First popularized in petting zoos, these miniatures are now growing in popularity as family pets.

Housing and Pasture for Sheep and Goats

While a barn is ideal, only minimal housing is needed for sheep and goats. A small shed or lean-to will do. The main thing is to provide a well-ventilated area that is dry, free of drafts, and safe from predators. Both straw and sawdust are good bedding materials. Goats are the gymnasts of the animal world. They like to climb and will appreciate rock piles and other elevated play areas. They also prefer to

All About Wool

Once a year (more in some parts of North America), you will need to remove the thick and fluffy frocks of sheep, alpacas, llamas, and angora goats. Shearing is usually performed in early spring. The animal must be dry before this process. Talk to local breeders or call your county agricultural agent to learn who performs this task in your area. You may also discover local demonstrations for those desiring to do this on their own.

Your pet's fleece is valuable to spinners, weavers, and knitters. If you do not have an interest in these crafts, talk to local breeders and your county extension agent about local wool markets.

Also keep in mind that your pet's woolly exterior may prevent you from noticing ticks or other external parasites. Consult local breeders and your veterinarian to develop a plan for controlling parasites.

rest on elevated surfaces. Sturdy objects that can be pushed around will be much appreciated.

Providing a protected outdoor area for these active animals can be a challenge. Choosing pygmy goats rather than a taller breed makes fencing easier, but the fence should still be tall enough to keep out predators such as coyotes. Goats of any height will squeeze between wires or boards. Woven wire fences work well for sheep but can be damaged by goats who like to push at the wire with their front feet. Goats can also get their horns stuck on wire fences, which will warp as the goat pulls itself loose. Make fences a minimum of 4.5 feet (137 centimeters) high for does and even higher for bucks (as goats are often jumpers). If wood is used, planks or slats must be close together and near the ground to prevent animals from squeezing through. Locks on gates need to be complicated enough to keep your curious pet secure. If your lock is too simple, a smart goat will be able to figure out how to let himself loose.

Pastured animals also need access to shade. Ideally, they will be able to enter the barn or shed from the pasture. Trees along a pasture edge only provide shade at certain times of the day. If no trees are located within the pasture, a few poles with a simple roof can serve as shelter from both rain and sun.

A large pasture with an ample supply of grass is the best thing you can offer your sheep and goats, but both can thrive without this as long as high-quality hay and grain are provided. Goats would rather eat hay from a manger than off the floor and may even refuse to bend down for this feed. Even kids as young as a week old should have access to a small amount of grain and hay. Goats will also appreciate access to a salt and mineral block. Be sure to locate this in an area protected from rain and snow. Provide leafy tree branches when possible. Avoid leaves from trees that have fruits with stones (plums, peaches, and cherries). When wilted, these leaves can poison your pets. With the exception of yew, which is toxic to goats, evergreens provide a welcome winter treat. Potatoes, carrots, and turnips are also healthy foods. If there are trees within your pasture that you would prefer your goats not strip of every branch and leaf within reach, build fences around those trees to keep your goats at a safe distance.

Llamas are becoming popular pets across North America.

Alpacas and Llamas

The common ancestor of alpacas and llamas is believed to have originated in North America and then traveled to South America, where human beings have depended on both for thousands of years. You can remember one historic difference between the animals by thinking of alpacas as "sheep of the Andes," as they have traditionally been raised for their wooly coats. So soft and luxurious is alpaca wool that it is sometimes referred to as the fiber of gods. Llamas were more like "ships of the Andes," because they were commonly used to carry loads.

The care and feeding of alpacas and llamas is much like that of sheep and goats. Like sheep, alpacas prefer grass. Like goats, llamas are browsers. Since llamas are tall, they can reach fairly high when eating. Commercial llama pellets are also available for feed.

Weighing anywhere from 100 to 175 pounds (45.4 to 79.4 kilograms), alpacas are usually hardy, gentle, and do not bite or butt. They also have a habit of using a common dung pile, which can make cleanup faster. Llamas, on the other hand, can grow to six feet (1.8 meters) tall and weigh between two hundred and four hundred pounds (90.7 to 181.4 kilograms). According to some breeders, handling male llamas too much when they are young can make them more aggressive to people once they are adults. Nonbreeding males of both species should be *gelded* when two years old. Male llamas should have their "fighting teeth" cut off when they are three. They are apt to bite at the knees and testicles of rival llamas, and aggressive individuals sometimes use similar tactics against other animals and people. They can also spit—a nasty habit if it is directed against you.

Alpacas come in twenty-two recognized colors and are called either suri or *huacaya* depending on the type of fiber they grow. The fluffy coat of huacaya (the most common) grows perpendicular to the animal's body. Suri fiber hangs down in ringlets. Huacaya fur is crimpy, but suri is smooth.

You will need to pay attention to your alpacas' and llamas' fur and hooves. Llamas do not get fleas, but ticks can be especially dangerous for them. Hoof problems can also prove dangerous to the animal's health. To guard against hoof rot, keep pets in dry areas. If hooves don't wear down enough from exercise, they need to be trimmed. Practice lifting the legs of young animals so they become accustomed to this activity. Because of their size, llamas may have to be placed in some type of restraint when having their hooves trimmed. Lame animals should be checked immediately for lodged stones. More serious problems demand consultation with a vet trained in the care of llamas and alpacas.

From Herding to Sledding: Rural Working Dogs

As in urban areas, dogs are one of the most popular pets in rural North America. Most are simply companions, but others have jobs to do. Some breeds have been employed as guardians of defenseless sheep for generations. The border collie is one of the most common herding breeds. Komondors, Great Pyrenees, Maremma sheepdogs, Kuvasz, Shar Planinetz, and Anatolian shepherds were also developed as herding dogs. Sometimes herding dogs compete in trials that are open to the public. You can also see both common and unusual breeds at American Kennel Club shows.

Herding is by no means the only job dogs have been bred to do in the country. Groups of Alaskan malamutes, huskies, and other dogs are still used for sledding in the northernmost parts of the United States and Canada. Though once essential for survival, sledding with the dogs is now mostly a fun hobby enjoyed by teens and adults.

Many of the animals kept as pets in rural areas were originally bred for other purposes. Sheep were useful for wool, milk, and meat. Goats were likewise useful for their milk and meat. Alpacas were raised for their wool. Llamas were used as beasts of burden. Yet another animal, the pig, was raised for **utilitarian** purposes long be-

Young border collies are often first taught to herd with geese or ducks, since a butt from an adult sheep might hurt a puppy.

fore it was considered as a pet. Today, however, you may be surprised to find that some rural youth are keeping pigs as pets as well. Long valued only as a source of chops, ribs, ham, and bacon, pigs are proving for many to be great animal companions.

CHAPTER 5
Here Piggy Piggy

"ELI THE PIG HOGGING ATTENTION AS HURST ELECTION NEARS"

"SUPPORT FOR ELI IS SLIM AT POLLS"

"DRINK-MAKER ASKS THAT PIG BE A PEPPER"

"BOTTLING COMPANY OFFERS REFUGE FOR ELI THE PIG"

"JURY FINDS PIG OWNER IN VIOLATION OF ORDINANCE"

"OWNERS MOVE ELI OUT OF CITY"

These are some of the articles that appeared in the *Star Telegram* of Hurst, Texas, between April and August of 2001, when a Dr. Pepper–loving pot-bellied pig named Eli became the focus of hot debate. In Hurst, where Eli lived, pigs were classified as livestock and restricted from living on lots smaller than one acre. Eli's owner, Cynthia Wynne, wanted him declared a pet. Roberta Womack formed a political action committee in opposition. When it came time for citizens to vote, Eli lost.

Domestic pigs have resided in North America since 1539. There are approximately three hundred pig breeds in the world today. Yorkshire, Duroc, and Hampshire are three of the most common types in the pork industry.

Between the 1960s and 1980s, a then-unusual member of the *Suidae* family began making its way from China and Vietnam to North American shores. A Canadian named Keith Connell first imported the animal for use in zoos and laboratories. Many people who had never warmed up to swine ownership before thought of this smaller *porcine* as unique, cute, and even desirable. Thus, potbellied pigs became North American pets. In fact, they became so popular that some people began referring to them as "Yuppie Puppies." Today there are more than a million pet pigs in North America, most of the "miniature" variety.

Though the word miniature is often used to describe potbellies, it is best to remember that this is a relative term. Potbellied pigs are miniature when compared to most other pigs. While selective breeding allows some potbellies to remain quite small, others can reach a full-grown weight of well over 150 pounds (68 kilograms). Potential owners must realize that these miniature pigs can be as heavy as our largest dogs—not a problem for many rural teens who can keep their pet outdoors, but a potential disaster for apartment-living urbanites.

Pigs are quite intelligent and can be loyal family pets. An episode of *Oprah* recounted how a pet pig saved the life of its owner when she suffered a heart attack. Realizing her owner needed help, the pig went outside and laid in the road until a car stopped. The pig then led the driver to her unconscious owner.

A pig and a peacock may be unusual pets—but like all pets, they require attention while they offer pleasure to their owners.

Light-skinned pigs are susceptible to sunburn.

The Nitty Gritty on Pig Ownership

Pigs that are less than eight weeks old are called piglets or suckling pigs. After that, they are called shoats or weaners—this is probably the age your pet will be at adoption. When they are older still, they are sometimes called runners. Young female pigs are gilts, and older ones are called sows. Neutered males are known as barrows; adult males kept for breeding are called boars.

Pigs can be housebroken and taught to use a doggie door (as long as the pig can fit through the opening). They can also be trained to use a litter box. Treat your indoor pig much as you would treat a dog, and provide a pet bed as a sleeping area. It can be amusing to take this eye-catching pet for a walk on a leash.

Pigs can certainly make unusual, rewarding, and loving pets, but be realistic when considering bringing one into your home. When the novelty wears off, reality will set in, and, as with all pets, you should be prepared for the realities of pig ownership before you commit to an animal. The workers at one pig rescue shelter that sometimes houses over a hundred animals do not advocate thinking of potbellied pigs as indoor pets. All too often, owners adopt an adorable piglet and are later surprised to find a full-grown pig opening cupboard doors and dumping garbage pails in the kitchen. If size is an important consideration for you, select a breeder known for producing pigs that consistently reach the height and weight you desire. You also need to be aware that pigs can have a life span of nearly twenty years, so be sure you are ready for a long-term commitment.

All pigs need outdoor exercise and access to enough ground to satisfy their rooting instincts. Training your pet to use a small, designated area with softened earth might save better parts of the lawn and even carpets from being exposed to this activity. Outdoor pigs need shelter that is dry and free of drafts. Failing to provide adequate housing can make the pig susceptible to pneumonia. Your pet can also acquire this sickness from infected pigs.

Indoor pigs usually need to have their hooves trimmed. Outdoor animals might accomplish this naturally with exercise on rough terrain. Males may also need their tusks trimmed regularly; if you wish to avoid this, choose a female. Have your pet spayed or neutered (when three months old for females, when three weeks old for males). The backbone of your pig-pal's diet should be a commercial feed specially formulated to meet a pig's nutritional needs. You should also provide your pig with a daily supply of fresh fruit and vegetables. Like a pet dog, there are many scraps your pig will be happy to clean off your plate.

Express Yourself

Pigs are among the most intelligent animals and can develop an impressive vocabulary of understood words. Remember, however, that all babies are born with a vocabulary of zero. Your animal friends will understand you better and develop their vocabularies quicker if you use expressive language when communicating with them. In other words, use your tone of voice and body language as tools to help the pet understand what you are saying. Use a soft and friendly tone when introducing yourself for the first time. Sound happy when praising a pet's good behavior. Speak with a commanding voice to indicate the pig must follow directions, and be kind but firm when correcting bad behavior. Potbellied pigs do not respond well to physical punishment.

Though pigs have hair, they're not really furry. Protect your pig from sunburn when outdoors. Make sure penned individuals have access to shade. You can also use a sunblock. Because pigs do not have sweat glands, care must be taken to protect them from extreme heat. Your pet pig might like to roll around in the mud to cool off on a hot day, but despite popular belief, pigs like to be as clean as any other animal. You will need to bathe your pet pig and groom it with a soft brush. Proper grooming can prevent troublesome skin conditions including *mange* and *seborrhea*. In cold weather, guard against frostbite. Potbellied pigs are reported to be nonshedding, *hy-*

poallergenic, and even odor-free. If the animal you are considering has an offensive odor, avoid this pig.

Signs that a vet visit is in Porky's best interest include either diarrhea or loss of appetite that lasts for more than a day. Constipation lasting for more than forty-eight hours is another reason for a trip to the vet. Rapid or labored breathing can be a warning sign that something is wrong. Unusual behavior, including excessive lying down or walking in a labored or wobbly manner, is cause for concern. Bumpy skin and blood in the pig's excrement are also signs that your pet is sick and needs medical attention. Like all pets, your pig will also need vaccinations.

Pigs may not be the first animals to pop into your mind when you think about a pet, but many people have found them to be great animal companions. Nevertheless, when it comes to rural youth and the pets they desire, perhaps the most *coveted* are still the horse and the pony. Although less popular and far more misunderstood, pet donkeys can also be found in rural areas.

CHAPTER 6
Miniature to Grand: Horses, Ponies, and Donkeys

"Can I remember my first riding experience? That's easy. It was on my uncle's farm when I was four. My uncle had a team of Percherons. Actually, he still has those horses. They were in the pulling contest here yesterday. Anyway, my uncle set my two cousins and me on Dolly's (that's one of the Percherons) back, climbed on up behind us, and took us for a ride. It was great for all of us to be up on that big back at the same time. I loved it. Ever since then, I've had a passion for horses. I've always loved the power, and now I crave the speed. Some people are scared of that, but I feel like I'm on top of the world when I'm skirting the barrels."

Tom Donaldson isn't the only teen who enjoyed horseback riding. Like Tom, many rural youth have a passion for horses.

Barrel racing and pulling contests are only two of the *equine* events that take place at county and state fairs across North America each year. Horsemen of all ages also enjoy taking horses through their paces in *dressage* and show-jumping competitions. Animals that don't participate in contests are enjoyed on trail rides or hitched to buggies and sleighs. Horses, ponies, and donkeys are working animals, and you need to consider many things before purchasing a specific one.

Age, Conformation, and Vices

When deciding to bring a horse, pony, or donkey into your family, it is usually best to purchase a well-trained animal. Leave younger individuals for experienced horsemen and trainers. Many horses and ponies are still athletic and capable of being ridden and enjoyed well into their twenties, and donkeys can live for thirty to fifty years.

Before purchase, you'll want to assess the animal's conformation—the form of the animal's body and how the animal moves. For example, the animal's legs and feet should be straight and should not knock together when it walks or runs. Animals with good form are said to be sound. This is what you are after. It can be difficult for a *novice* to assess conformation. Read books and take every opportunity to view animals while stabled and in action to learn what to look for. If possible, have horses, ponies, and donkeys assessed by an experienced horseman before purchase.

Know the animal's history. Members of the horse family are smart and have long memories. Bad experiences can leave lasting impressions that take the form of quirks and vices. A horse that has

Horses are social animals. They need animal companions—either other horses or a goat or sheep—or they will be lonely.

Like all animals, donkeys, ponies, and horses have unique temperaments. Some are not an ideal match for children and young adults—but many are sweet-tempered and gentle.

gotten stuck in a small space in a barn may develop a fear of walking through narrow gates, for example, or it might spook when parts of the saddle knock against its sides. An animal who has stumbled down a hill near a culvert could now be afraid of all culverts and fight its rider every time one has to be crossed. This is not to say that animals like this should never be purchased, but you should try to make all such discoveries in advance so that you know what you might expect.

An animal that paws the ground and stomps around in an aggressive manner is cause for concern. Avoid any that kick or bite. An animal that continuously shifts its weight from one foreleg to the other and swings its head from one side to the other should also be avoided.

Other Considerations

Determine exactly what it is you want to accomplish with a horse, pony, or donkey before looking at potential pets. Take riding or driving lessons at a local stable, attend shows, and ride or drive as many animals as possible. Become educated regarding breeds, including their availability, expense, and care. Look into the cost of necessary *tack*, clothing, transportation, and entry fees for activities of interest.

Discuss your hopes and plans with your family. Make sure you have the facilities to house and feed the intended pet. Be certain fencing is strong enough to sustain the weight of a horse pushing against it. (This is not necessary with electric fencing since the shock will discourage the animal.) Purchase the following before the animal arrives at its new home:

- basic grooming supplies (brush, rubber curry comb, and hoof pick)

- bedding materials (straw or sawdust)

- equipment for cleaning the stall (pitchfork for straw, metal rake for sawdust, shovel, and wheelbarrow)

- feed (hay and oats or sweet feed, an oats and molasses mixture)

- water buckets

Think before purchasing a stallion (called a jack in the donkey world), since they are less reliable and harder to handle. Ride or drive mares (called jennets for donkeys) and geldings before purchase. If that goes well, ask to lead the animal to the stable and groom it there. Notice how the current owner ties the horse, pony, or donkey. You may want to set up a similar system in your barn.

Donkeys and horses enjoy carrots as a treat, but most of their nutrition should come from hay and grain.

Speak to the animal gently as you assist in tack removal and begin grooming. Have the owner demonstrate how she picks up each of the animal's feet for cleaning and how she brushes the tail.

Feeding

Horses, ponies, and donkeys can be kept in barnyards without access to pasture, but pasturing during snow-free months is the preferable situation. Not only does it improve the animal's quality of life and provide important opportunities for exercise, pasturing also cuts down on the need for hay.

The amount of grain a horse, pony, or donkey requires depends on the animal and its activities. Horses usually need oats or sweet feed twice each day, and they require more grain in winter than in summer. Grain is not always given to donkeys. Consult your breeder and veterinarian to determine a good ration for your particular pet. A salt and mineral block should be provided, but horses, ponies, and donkeys should never have access to a salt block formulated for goats or cattle. Place hay on the ground but feed grain from a container. If you have more than one horse, pony, or donkey, separate the animals during feeding so that one cannot dominate and steal food from the other. Your horse, pony, or donkey will enjoy occasional apples and carrots, but too many can be dangerous. It is best to cut treats into pieces to avoid choking. Take care that fruit trees and dropped fruit are out of reach when fencing a pasture.

Access to water must be available at all times. To prevent overturned buckets, attach the bucket handle to a hook on the stable wall or use a bucket insulator—a bucket holder that is bolted to the wall. Bucket insulators have the advantage of preventing water from freezing in cold weather, something you may greatly appreciate if the alternative is trudging through a foot of snow a couple of times a day to replace a frozen water supply. Scrub food and water containers weekly.

Diseases and Parasites

Having fewer pets, especially of the same breed, minimizes most disease and parasite problems. In other words, the more contact your pet has with others of its own type, the more likely it will catch something. But it seems unfair to deprive an animal of visiting with others, and many rural teens want to show their animals in competition. Before exhibiting your pet, find out what precautions competition organizers take to minimize exposure to disease, and be sure to follow the precautions yourself to minimize others' risk of contracting something from your own animal. Here are some basic steps you should take to promote good sanitation and proper management of parasites and other health problems.

- Separate animals from manure as much as possible, and dispose of excrement quickly.

- Prevent environmental stress by rotating pastures if possible and protecting pets from weather extremes.

- Do not house animals in damp conditions or pasture them in swampy areas.

- Keep food and water fresh and clean.

- Make sure grain and other food supplies are sealed in appropriate containers, and take other necessary measures to control rodent infestations.

- Regularly wash housing and feeding utensils with a stiff brush and appropriate cleansers.

- Avoid drafts but ensure good ventilation.

- Equines are susceptible to internal parasites and need to be on a worming schedule.

- A series of inoculations against diseases is necessary. Consult your vet accordingly.

- Be alert to changes in animal behavior or condition, call your veterinarian when necessary, and act quickly to restore good health.

General Equine Care

The more you ride or drive your pet, the healthier and more accustomed to these activities it will be. Like all athletes, horses, ponies, and donkeys should be warmed up before strenuous exercise and cooled down afterward. Daily brushing also allows you to spend quality time bonding with your pet, calms the animal, and keeps it accustomed to handling. This important activity also promotes health and allows you to notice any ticks, lice, or injuries.

Equine teeth grow throughout the life of the animal. These animals grind their food when they chew, and this wears at their teeth. Ideally, the teeth should wear evenly, but sharp edges sometimes occur or the teeth do not meet correctly. If you notice food falling from the animal's mouth or suspect it is in discomfort from a tooth problem, take a look or call a vet to inspect the animal's mouth. Sometimes it is necessary for the vet to file sharp edges. This procedure is called floating.

Protect equines against annoying and unhealthy flies during warm months. Animals that have constant access from the pasture to the barn can stable themselves when necessary to get away from these insects or from inclement weather. You can also wipe your pet down with a commercial bug repellent formulated for equine use or cover your pet with a fly net. Donkeys usually tolerate flies better than horses and ponies. In addition to protection from insects, light-colored horses and *chestnuts* may need a sunblock to protect against burns.

Horses need to be curried to keep their coats shiny.

Regular hoof care is essential. Ask equine owners in your area to recommend a farrier—a professional who can trim your equine's hooves and shoe the animal if necessary. Unlike horses and ponies, donkeys don't usually need shoes.

Like sheep and goats, horses, ponies, and donkeys are herd animals. In the wild, they live in groups and have complex social relationships. Sociable animals like these suffer in isolation. They prefer to be housed with another equine. In the absence of that possibility, however, they will usually accept a sheep, goat, or other animal. It should be noted that donkeys tend to dislike dogs, having a strong instinct to defend against canine predators. They may attack dogs, causing injury or even death. Donkeys and dogs that are raised together from the time they are very young may get along just fine. If you already have a canine in the household, it may take time and patience to successfully introduce it to a donkey.

Rent-a-Horse

Horses are expensive pets. You may want to test your desire for long-term ownership by first renting or borrowing an animal. Riding stables may be able to put you in touch with an owner who wishes to rent out an animal. Contact local summer camps that keep horses. They may be willing to loan out animals when schools are in session (up to nine months of the year) in exchange for care and feeding.

From chickens to goats, pigs to horses, the pets commonly found in rural areas require specific types of care. No matter what type of pet you have, however, there are other general considerations you must keep in mind. For instance, who will take care of your pet when you go on vacation? What would happen to your pet if you had to move? How long is your pet's lifespan, and what emotions will you face when your pet dies? These are questions to ask when you are considering pet ownership, and it's important to think about your current life circumstances and how they might change in the future before inviting a new pet into your home.

CHAPTER 7
Changing Circumstances

One of the biggest challenges that can come with the types of rural pets discussed here is that unlike dogs and cats, these pets must stay home when their human family goes on vacation. This means that pet-care arrangements must be made prior to a family departing for more than a day at a time. Professional pet sitters can be hard to find in rural areas. Friends and neighbors who already know the animal often make excellent pet sitters.

When arranging for someone to care for your pet, make sure he has had a demonstration of all necessary care he is expected to provide. Show the pet sitter exactly how much food needs to be provided at each meal, and stress the need for a constant supply of fresh water. Explain exactly when he must care for the pet—most animals become accustomed to their feeding schedule, and interruptions to the schedule can lead to hunger, unhappiness, and unruly behavior—and provide information on how to contact you during your absence. Remember to also get their contact information. Write down all care instructions (including those for any medications that might need to be given), your contact information, and the veterinarian's telephone number; and show the pet sitter where this will be posted for reference. Have him pet the animal, speak to it, and feed it in your presence so you can reassure the animal that this is a friend who will care for it until your return. Make certain that the caregiver and the animal feel comfortable with each other.

If you can't find a pet sitter who will come to the animal, perhaps you can bring the animal to the sitter. Look for a trusted friend who will care for the animal at her home, and arrange to bring the pet there on a visit prior to your trip. Be sure to decide how your pet will be introduced (if compatible animals are involved) or kept separate from pets at the temporary home.

If neither of these options is available, locate a kennel or stable willing to house your pet. If your pet has serious health issues, see if the veterinarian has boarding facilities. Ask your veterinarian and friends for recommendations. Be certain all vaccinations are up to date before allowing your pet to come into contact with other animals.

Traveling with Pets

If you will be traveling with your pet, whether on vacation or for show or competition purposes, there are certain preparations you should take. Make sure your pet is accustomed to traveling before taking it on a long trip. Check ahead of time with all relatives, hotels, resorts, and other places you plan to visit to be certain the pet will be welcome and have appropriate accommodations.

Pack enough of the animal's usual feed and special treats to last the trip. It's also a good idea to take some of your pet's regular water to ease the transition to strange water. Remember you'll also need food and water dishes. Don't travel with a sick pet. If your pet gets an upset stomach when traveling, consult the veterinarian for a remedy. Do not feed animals immediately before leaving, and be certain to carry enough paper towels, sanitary wipes, and other necessary equipment for an emergency cleanup should your animal get sick or unexpectedly relieve itself.

Small animals should always be placed in a carrier or specially designed car seat. Place a harness or collar with identification on the pet, and stop frequently to walk the animal on a leash. To prevent a tragedy, always leash the pet before opening the vehicle door. Likewise, remove the leash after the door is closed. Never leave an unattended animal in a car. The temperature in cars can rise extremely quickly. In a matter of moments, a car can get hot enough to cause heatstroke and even death.

Even pets that rarely travel must occasionally make a trip to the vet. Always place animals in secure carriers. Pets that are roaming freely about a vehicle can distract the driver, obscure her vision, or possibly even interfere with access to gas and brake pedals. Use seat belts to secure carriers. If the animal is too large for a carrier, use another appropriate restraint such as a net or steel barrier.

If it is too hot to drive with the window completely up, open it only slightly. You never know when something might catch your pet's attention and it decides to investigate further, jumping out of the window and possibly into oncoming traffic. Don't let your animals ride in the back of trucks unless they are in secured carriers. You might think it's cute and fun for your pet (and your pet might think it's a hoot), but it can be extremely dangerous to your pet.

All animals will need
occasional medical visits.

Unsecured, it can jump out of the truck and be injured. Even secured, severe jostling or an accident can injure them significantly.

Large pets, such as horses and llamas, need to be transported in
trailers made specifically for this purpose. Most rural areas have
large-animal vets who will come to your home to provide medical
treatment.

Letting Go

No matter how much we love our pets, sometimes we have to say
goodbye. Most families are able to bring their small pets when relo-
cating to a new home because of a job change or other reasons. But
sometimes, especially if the family is moving a great distance or
leaving a rural area for a more urban one, it may not be possible for

a large pet to move with them. If they are switching from a rural area to a city, some animals classified as livestock might be restricted. Even when moving to the countryside, the amount of property at the new home or the lack of animal-friendly accommodations could make the inclusion of certain pets impossible.

If you must find a new home for a beloved pet, talk to friends and family first. By giving a pet to someone you know, you can have a greater awareness of the type of home and care the new pet owner will provide. If, however, none of your friends and family are interested in taking in a new animal companion, call your vet and explain your situation. She may be able to put you in contact with individuals who have been seeking a certain type of pet. Contact a rescue organization for your type of pet. Information about breed-specific rescues can be found on the Internet. In many cases, your pet will be placed in a loving foster home until it can be rehomed in a permanent placement. Most rescue groups carefully screen all potential adopters to help ensure a transition to a loving and caring home. Some require a vet reference as well as personal references. An animal sanctuary can also be a solution to rehoming a pet. Information about these is also available on the Internet. People who work at animal shelters may also be able to provide you with the names of people interested in adopting a pet.

As a last resort, you may decide to advertise in the newspaper. If you must pursue this option, do everything possible to learn what type of a home your pet will be going to. Advertise well in advance of your move to give yourself time to investigate fully all your pet's options. Have interested persons visit the pet at your home. Explain all that is involved in caring for the animal. If you decide the individual or family might be a good match, offer to bring the animal to their home for a visit prior to your final decision.

After the decision is made, write down all special needs, favorite foods, vet contact information, and your new telephone number, and give it to the new owner. To make this as easy on the pet as possible, provide the new owner with your pet's food dishes, special toys, and as much other equipment as is possible and practical. Also provide some of your pet's favorite food and litter if possible. Having familiar things around him will help in the transition process.

Dealing with Grief

Welcoming a new pet into your home is a joyous experience. Whether your pet is large or small, lives indoors or outdoors, you will hopefully have a mutually fulfilling relationship for many years. Since most animals we keep as pets have a shorter life span than humans, however, there will eventually come a time when you must say goodbye to your pet. Experiencing the death of a beloved pet can be agonizing, and thinking ahead of time about what you will do if your pet gets sick or dies can help prepare you for the day when you must say goodbye.

Sometimes animals develop painful and untreatable illnesses. When untreatable pain is involved and recovery is impossible, the kindest act may be to have the pet *euthanized*. Making this decision is usually traumatic. When recovery is impossible but the pet is not in pain, many pet owners decide to keep their pet as comfortable as possible while allowing it to have a natural death.

Discuss all options with your family and veterinarian. If euthanasia (usually accomplished by injection of a lethal substance) seems like the best path, consider staying with the pet during this procedure. It will comfort the animal, and although it may be emotionally draining for you at the time, you might feel better later to have seen that your pet died quickly, painlessly, and surrounded by the people who loved him and who he loved. Saying good-bye to the pet either before or after the injection and leaving the room when the drug is administered is another option, and there is no reason to feel or be made to feel that this is the wrong thing to do. Some vets will come to your home to administer the injection, allowing your pet to die in familiar surroundings.

Saying good-bye is never easy.

It is natural to feel sad and depressed when separating from a pet. Allow yourself to grieve. It can be helpful to share feelings with family, friends, trusted teachers, or the guidance counselor or psychologist at your school. Some vet hospitals have **bereavement** groups to help you deal with the loss of your pet.

Some people decide that since a pet's death will eventually cause heartache, it's better not to get a pet at all. If you are inclined to feel this way, think carefully before completely ruling a pet out of your life. For some people, forgoing pet ownership may indeed be the right decision. For others, however, the benefits of pet ownership—from learning responsibility to giving and receiving unconditional love—far outweigh any drawbacks.

All kinds of opportunities for animal companionship are out there. From the most popular pets—dogs and cats—to the more unusual like pigs and alpacas, with proper research, time, and commitment, rural teens can find the pet best suited to their personality, lifestyle, and home.

Further Reading

Bennett, Bob. *Rabbits as a Hobby*. Neptune City, N.J.: TFH Publications, 1992.

Dwelle, Jacqueline. *Your First Horse: How to Buy and Care for Your First Horse*. Southern Pines, N.C.: Hoofbeat Publications, 1996.

Fischer, Arlene, and Herbert A. Nieberg. *Pet Loss: A Thoughtful Guide for Adults and Children*. New York: HarperCollins, 1996.

Ford, Peter. *Home Farm Handbook: A Comprehensive Guide to Buying, Raising, and Breeding Farm Animals Successfully*. Hauppauge, N.Y.: Barron's Educational Series, Inc., 2000.

Hall Huckaby, Lisa. *Pot-Bellied Pigs and Other Miniature Pet Pigs*. Neptune City, N.J.: TFH Publications, 1992.

Hanna, Jack, with Hester Mundis. *Jack Hanna's Ultimate Guide to Pets*. New York: G. P. Putnam's Sons, 1996.

Harriot, James. *James Herriot's Animal Stories*. New York: St. Martin's Press, 1997.

Holderread, Dave. *Raising Ducks*. Pownal, Vt.: Storey Books, 2000.

Mercia, Leonard S. *Storey's Guide to Raising Poultry: Breeds, Care, Health*. Pownal, Vt.: Storey Books, 2000.

Rath, Sara. *The Complete Pig: An Entertaining History of Pigs*. Stillwater, Minn.: Voyageur Press, Inc., 2000.

Roberts, Monty. *The Man Who Listens to Horses*. New York: Random House, 1997.

Simmons, Paula, and Carol Ekarius. *Storey's Guide to Raising Sheep: Breeds, Care, Facilities*. Pownal, Vt.: Storey Books, 2000.

Smith, Mike. *Getting the Most from Riding Lessons*. Pownal, Vt.: Storey Books, 1998.

Smith, Sharon B. *The Affordable Horse: A Guide to Low-Cost Ownership*. New York: Howell Book House, 1994.

Tarte, Bob. *Enslaved by Ducks: How One Man Went From Head of the Household to Bottom of the Pecking Order*. Chapel Hill, N.C.: Algonquin Books of Chapel Hill, 2003.

Valentine, Priscilla. *Potbellied Pig Behavior and Training*. Pullman, Wash.: Luminary Media Group, 2000.

For More Information

Alpaca and llama information
www.islandnet.com/~morlan/history.html

The American Donkey and Mule Society
www.lovelongears.com

The American Livestock Breeds Conservancy
This nonprofit organization works to protect more than a hundred rare breeds
of cattle, poultry, sheep, goats, pigs, horses, and donkeys.
http://albc-usa.org/wtchlist.htm

American Rabbit Breeders Association, Inc.
P. O. Box 426
Bloomington, IL 61702
www.arba.net

American Veterinary Medical Association
www.avma.org

Best Friends Animal Society
5001 Angel Canyon Road
Kanab, UT 84741-5000
www.bestfriends.org

Care for My Horse
www.care-for-my-horse.com

Miniature Horse information
www.theminiaturehorse.com

Murray McMurray Hatchery: common poultry breeds and the world's largest
rare breed hatchery
www.mcmurrayhatchery.com

The National Animal Poison Control Center
University of Illinois
(888) 426-4435
www.anapsid.org/resources/napcc.html

Pigs: A Sanctuary
www.pigs.org

Publisher's note:
The Web sites listed on this page were active at the time of publication. The publisher is not responsible for Web sites that have changed their addresses or dis-
continued operation since the date of publication. The publisher will review and
update the Web-site list upon each reprint.

Glossary

abscesses: Pus-filled cavities resulting from inflammation and usually caused by a bacterial infection.

avian: Relating to, belonging to, or characteristic of birds.

bereavement: The lose of a loved one by death.

Bovidae: Family name of hollow-horned, hoofed animals that includes cattle, sheep, and antelopes.

chestnuts: Reddish-brown horses.

coveted: Wanted something very strongly.

crop: A pouch in the gullet of many birds where they store partially digested food before regurgitating it to feed their young.

culled: Removed a sickly or weak animal from a herd or flock.

domesticated: Cultivated, raised, or bred for human needs.

dressage: A competitive event where horse and rider are judged on the elegance, precision, and discipline of a horse's movement.

equine: Belonging to or characteristic of the family of mammals that include horses, zebras, and donkeys.

euthanized: Killed an incurably ill or injured animal in a humane way to relieve its suffering.

foragers: Animals who search for food.

free-range: Animals allowed to move and feed at will, rather than being confined to a pen.

gelded: Castrated.

gregarious: Very friendly and sociable.

homing instincts: The instinctual ability of some animals to find their way home after traveling a long distance.

hypoallergenic: Not likely to cause an allergic reaction.

inclement: Bad, especially in relation to weather.

lesions: Areas of skin that are broken or infected.

listless: Lacking energy, interest, or the willingness to make an effort to do something.

mange: An infectious skin disease caused by mites that results in hair loss, scabs, and itching.

neutering: Removing the testicles or ovaries of an animal.

novice: Someone who is inexperienced.

pastoral: Relating to the countryside or rural life.

plumage: The feathers that cover a bird's body.

porcine: Relating to pigs.

pullet: A young female chicken who has not started to lay eggs.

resins: Natural organic substances secreted in the sap of some plants and trees.

roughage: Food containing indigestible material.

seborrhea: Excessively oily skin caused by heavy discharge from the sebaceous glands.

spaying: Surgically removing an animal's ovaries and adjacent parts of the uterus.

status symbol: A possession that shows a sign of wealth or prestige.

stave: To keep or hold off; repell.

Suidae: Old World pigs.

tack: Saddles, bridles, and other parts of a horse's harness.

utilitarian: Designed for practical use.

vermin: Small, common, harmful, or objectionable animals that are difficult to control.

wanes: Gradually decreases in intensity or power.

wean: To start feeding a young animal food other than its mother's milk.

zoning laws: Regulations that outline the types of residential and commercial activities that can be conducted in a defined area.

Index

alpaca 47, 50, 56, 58, 59, 89
American Rabbit Breeders Association 45

birds 11, 17, 19, 27, 31, 43
    babies 19, 20, 21, 23
    care of 15, 21, 25, 26, 27
    egg production 25
    feeding 24
    health of 22, 23, 24
    housing 23
    purchasing 19, 20, 22, 23

cats 9, 10, 11, 23, 40, 46, 83, 89
chickens 17, 19, 20, 22, 23, 24, 25, 27, 31, 81
chicks 10, 20, 21

dogs 9, 10, 11, 23, 35, 35, 40, 41, 47, 60, 64, 67, 80, 83, 89
donkeys 69, 72, 75, 76, 77, 79, 70,
ducks 20, 23, 26, 27, 31, 61

ferrets 10, 40

geese 20, 23, 26, 27, 28, 31, 61
goats 47, 50, 52, 53, 54, 55, 56, 57, 59, 60, 73, 77, 80, 81
guinea fowl 19, 31

horses 50, 69, 72, 81, 86
    care of 75, 79, 80
    feeding 76, 77
    purchasing 72
    renting 81

kittens 10, 40

llamas 47, 50, 56, 58, 59, 86

North America 10, 33, 50, 56, 58, 60, 64, 72

peacocks 17, 19, 65
pesticides 17
pheasants 19, 30, 31
pigeons 28, 29, 30
pigs 63, 64, 81, 89
    breeds 64
    care of 67, 68
    health 14, 67, 69
    in houses 66, 67
    piglets 66, 67
    potbellied 64, 67, 68
    rescue shelters 67
    uses of 60, 61, 64
ponies 69, 72, 75, 76, 77, 79, 80
puppies 10, 40, 61, 64

quail 19, 31

rabbits 11, 31, 33, 43, 47
    care of 34, 37, 40, 42
    choosing 40, 41, 42
    feeding 43, 44
    health of 38, 39, 43, 45, 46, 47
    housing 34, 35, 36, 37
    registration 45
    thumping 36
    wool 46

sheep 47, 49, 50, 52, 53, 55, 56, 57, 59, 60, 61, 73, 80

Picture Credits

Biographies

Author

Joyce Libal is a graduate of the University of Wisconsin. In addition to having worked as a magazine editor, she has written several books for adolescents. Joyce and her family have enjoyed raising many pets including chickens, geese, rabbits, dogs, cats, horses, and a pony on their Pennsylvania farm.

Series Consultant

Celeste J. Carmichael is a 4-H Youth Development Program Specialist at the Cornell University Cooperative Extension Administrative Unit in Ithaca, New York. She provides leadership to statewide 4-H Youth Development efforts including communications, curriculum, and conferences. She communicates the needs and impacts of the 4-H program to staff and decision makers, distributing information about issues related to youth and development, such as trends for rural youth.